MY KIND OF POETRY

MY KIND OF POETRY

Janice Carter

Best wishes

Janice Carter

ARTHUR H. STOCKWELL LTD
Torrs Park, Ilfracombe, Devon, EX34 8BA
Established 1898
www.ahstockwell.co.uk

ISBN 978-0-7223-4769-0
Printed in Great Britain by
Arthur H. Stockwell Ltd
Torrs Park   Ilfracombe
Devon   EX34 8BA

DEDICATION

I would like to dedicate this book in memory of Mum and Dad, and two dear friends I lost in 2014, Galyna, aged forty, and Lil, aged fifty-nine.

This is a book of mostly light-hearted poems, about people I know and have worked with, places I've been and also famous people that I like! I hope you enjoy reading it.

I would like to thank family, friends, work colleagues and the famous people included in this book.

Thanks once again.

Janice Carter

CONTENTS

MAGNIFICENT NORWAY

Magnificent Norway,
Land of the Midnight Sun,
Astounds you with beauty and peace,
Laughter and fun.

Its deep, long fjords,
And mountains so vast,
You think of longboats
And Vikings of the past.

Enchantment surrounds you
Wherever you go
As the spring sunshine
Glistens on the snow.

Everywhere waterfalls
Tumbling free,
Down to the fjords
And out to the sea.

Quaint wooden churches,
Hiding in the trees,
Standing so proud,
Saying, "Look at me, please."

The silence and beauty
Give you peace of mind,
But I must go home
And leave it behind.

This holiday has memories
The years will never fade,
Majestic and beautiful,
Magnificent Norway.

JERSEY

Jersey is my island
In the sun,
The quiet of the country
And the town is full of fun.

The people are friendly,
So happy and gay.
They make you welcome,
To enjoy your stay.

Stroll the sandy beaches,
See the magic of Corbière.
It's far beyond one's reach,
Just like floating on air.

The silent hush of the bay,
As the sun sets over the sea,
But I'll return one day
To the island that's part of me.

ST GEORGE'S DAY

St George killed the dragon,
Or so they say,
And now we celebrate
St George's Day.

We're proud to be British
Through and through,
Whatever we wish,
Whatever we do.

So put out the flags
For St George's Day,
Stand up and shout,
"Hip hip hooray!"

WONDERFUL WALES

Wonderful Wales –
They speak with a different tongue.
In the valleys and vales
There's a song to be sung.

There's male voice choirs,
Daffodils and leeks.
The singing's full of fire
When the dragon speaks.

It's where we belong,
Full of mystery and tales,
They call it the Land of Song –
That's wonderful Wales.

BONNIE SCOTLAND

Bonnie Scotland,
That's what they say –
Haggis, pipes, bands
And a whisky for every day.

There's lochs and mountains,
Fishing for salmon and trout,
Lots of castles and fountains,
And then there's a monster about.

So come and see the heather,
And travel around the glens.
It's not so hot on the weather,
But there's lots of kilted men.

So what does a Scotsman wear?
Ever wondered what's underneath?
Are they completely bare?
Oh! Tartan knickers! That's a relief.

SWINDON TOWN

Swindon was a railway town
For many, many years.
When it closed for good
There was anger and lots of tears.

With it went the hooter,
No railwaymen to call;
Now it's in the museum,
Quiet once and for all.

Now it's the Magic Roundabout
That people come to see.
Not the one on the telly,
With Dougal, Florence and Zebedee!

Film star Diana Dors,
Here in Swindon she was born,
From small-town beginnings
To take Hollywood by storm.

So if you visit Swindon,
Of which I am very fond,
See old and new-shaped buildings
Which appear in films of James Bond!

HIGHWORTH, 2010

It's Highworth's Year of Culture,
So let's have lots of fun.
The year is 2010 –
It really has begun.

Culture is a small word,
But certainly means a lot
For a small town like Highworth,
So let's see what we've got.

With the Thames close by
There's lots to see and do,
And a wealth of history
Unfolds before you.

Highworth is a hill town
With splendid views around.
You can spot three counties –
Quite charming, I've found.

RICHARD WILSON: A TOUCH OF MAGIC

What a comedy actor!
You've got to be the best.
There's a star on your door,
Never mind the rest.

Richard, you were brave
To take on such a part.
With *One Foot in the Grave*
The nation took you to heart.

You've had a share of hits
With *Only When I Laugh*!
And *Tutti Frutti* too.
"I just don't believe it!"
There's no limit to what you do.

I enjoyed the antique glamour
Of *Under the Hammer*,
A Sharp Intake of Breath
And *Carry on Columbus*, no less.

The Other Side of Paradise,
Crown Court and *Fatherland*.
A Passage to India,
Which was really rather grand!

You must be in *Who's Who*,
Since you took TV by storm,
Fame has never changed you
In any shape or form.

What an honour it must be,
For your service to the theatre
To receive an OBE.
You deserve it – every letter.

DAVID STARKEY: MAN AND HIS MONARCHY

I enjoy your programmes on TV –
You present them very well –
On the history of the monarchy
And the stories they could tell.

If you could choose
One person to meet
From history's who's who,
Who would you like to greet?

Or go back in time,
Be invisible to all,
Back to the Tudor line,
You'll have a ball.

But don't lose your head!
You're still fit and able –
You'll be well fed
At King Henry's table.

If he could look around
Our busy world today
With all the sights and sounds,
"I don't believe it!" he'd say.

I hope you like
This little rhyme –
I might make history
Of my own in time.

BARGAIN HUNT

I love watching *Bargain Hunt* –
I watch it every day
To see what the contestants buy
And what the experts say.

Tim, I like your style –
Waistcoats, scarves and dicky bows.
Everything matches,
Even the glasses that rest on your nose.

There's lots of lovely things,
But time's running out.
Shall we buy this or that?
"Time's up," Tim's about to shout.

With the leftover lolly,
What will the experts buy?
Sometimes it's a novelty
And sometimes you could cry.

Visiting historic houses
For a glimpse into the past;
Then it's back to the auction house,
Ready for the off at last.

It's a fun programme
With teams red and blue.
Will they make a profit,
And how much if they do?

So keep on bargain hunting,
And if you're a likely pair
Who enjoy an antique rummage
Then enter if you dare.

TERRY GRIFFITHS

Here's to the champ
Of seventy-nine.
We hope you like
This little rhyme.

Blondie of the tables,
Snooker is your game.
We know that you're quite able
'Cause it's your claim to fame.

So sip your coke
And chalk your cue.
Snooker us folk
With what you do!

Your talented gift
And the winning frame –
The trophy you'll lift,
To be champion again.

RICHARD ANGWIN

You're our local weatherman.
You read it very well.
Sometimes it's a mystery,
And very hard to tell.

Come sunshine or rain,
You always appear,
And try to tell us
What we want to hear.

So when it rains
Or when it snows
You can always say,
"I told you so!"

When the sun comes out,
You smile and say,
"Look up to the sky –
It's a lovely day."

Keep reading the weather,
We won't make a fuss.
You've got lots of fans,
So stay west with us!

JOHN, THE MILKMAN

Thanks for bringing the milk,
And the good job you do
In all kinds of weather.
A merry Christmas to you.

So in the New Year,
Keep doing the rounds,
Up and down doorsteps
In leaps and bounds.

Be careful round the drive –
Odd people live up here.
You will survive!
So have no fear.

Enjoy your Christmas
With family and mates.
Don't overdo it –
Have a couple of milkshakes!

SUPER STEVE

Up at the crack of dawn,
Gardening's your job,
Cutting trees, hedges and lawns –
Anything to earn a bob.

Growing different veggies
Along with beans and peas,
Not so keen trimming hedges
But do your best to please.

Cutting off the dead heads –
Good job they're not alive.
Planting all the flower beds,
You hope that they'll survive.

Digging up the ground
With your fork and spade,
Is it treasure you've found,
Looking into the hole you made?

Guess what keeps coming through?
Nothing but weed after weed.
Go home – there's plenty to do;
You've got the birds to feed.

THE BUTCHER OF STRATTON

In our local butcher's shop
Is where we get our meat.
It's also a one-to-one stop
And the counter's really neat.

The butcher, Paul,
Loves blood and gore
Films like *Hannibal*,
Seven and *Saw*.

Good morning. What's for dinner?
How about a beef roast?
Not a piece of the winner –
First past the post.

When I pop in
His chopper comes out.
"I'll have some griskin.
That's enough," I'll shout.

Pat takes the money –
She loves a Carry On
The films were very funny;
Now all the stars have gone.

Pat can name them all
So take your pick:
There's *Carry On Henry*,
Cleo, *Jack* and *Dick*!

If you want to risk it
Come in and you can buy
One side a bit of brisket,
The other a custard pie.

DAZZLING DARREN

Your job is window cleaning
All over, and Derwent Drive.
You also watch birds preening –
It keeps you happy and alive.

I mean birds of a feather
That fly and nest in trees,
Not the birds wearing leather –
The ones eager to please.

Looking through the glass
I bet you've seen some sights.
Has anyone made a pass?
That would give you a fright.

You have to stop and stare
When cleaning off the glass.
Oh, what a lovely pair
Of blue tits, just flown past.

Now the windows are clean
It's improved our viewing.
We can see where you've been
And what you've been doing.

WALL 2 WALL

Paper, paint and paste,
That's wall to wall,
Finished just to your taste.
Why not give them a call?

They paint round windows,
Ceilings and doors,
Hang your wallpaper,
And lots, lots more.

Jan's the leader
Of a winning team,
And when they leave
It's nice and clean.

With overalls nearly white
And with all the gear!
New paint is nice and bright,
Then the old will disappear.

With paint pots and brushes,
They're professional you know.
Could it be someone like Rembrandt
Or maybe Michelangelo!

Michelangelo (1475-1564)? No!
Wrong moment in time.
Of course it's Janet Angelo –
That fits in with the rhyme.

THE SINGING BUILDER

The singing builder
Does it all.
Pick up the phone –
Give him a call.

If you want a conservatory,
New roof and some doors,
He'll do the lot
And tile the floors.

He'll pave your drive
And build a wall,
Mend pipes and drains
And that's not all.

That's his day job;
What about night?
He'll take the mic and sing!
That'll give you a fright!

"Give us a song!"
That's what they say –
A cowboy by night,
But not by day.

He enjoys his singing,
So put yourself about.
You never know who's watching –
Maybe a talent scout!

When he's on the roof
He might give you a song –
If I were a rich man
I'd be long gone.

That's the singing builder –
Roy's the name.
Jack of all trades
His claim to fame.

THE HAIRDRESSER

Hairdressing's an art
With scissors and combs,
Rollers, nets
And lots of foam.

There's ginger redheads,
Dark hair and fair,
Blondes, brunettes
And some without hair.

Try a new style –
It could be fun.
Have a razor cut,
Pageboy, or bun.

There's pigtails, ponytails,
Ringlets that twirl,
Long hair and short,
Some that just curl.

Try colouring your hair
Blue, pink or green –
Now, that's something
Your grannie's never seen.

In years gone by
You just went grey.
There was no dye
Like there is today.

Without a hairdresser
Where would we be?
All wearing wigs –
What a sight to see!

A VISIT TO THE DENTIST

No one likes the dentist –
It's something you have to do!
You have to look after your teeth,
And then they'll look after you.

You look around the room –
Could this be the electric chair?
It's all doom and gloom –
Sit down if you dare!

Maybe it's just a check,
Or it could be a filling.
Then you'll feel like a wreck,
After all that drilling.

Oh! This tooth's gone bad.
You give out a shout:
"It's driving me mad!"
"Then let's take it out!"

Now just a scale and polish,
And they'll look super-white.
They've not all been demolished;
It's all turned out just right.

"That's it for today."
You come out with a smile.
"See you again," you say –
I hope not for a while.

SmiLE

A FISHERMAN'S FRIEND

Ken's a man who loves fishing
And sits on the bank all day,
Quietly hoping and wishing
A big fish would come his way!

Some people think it's odd
Sat waiting for a bite,
Staring down at your rod –
Then suddenly the line gets tight!

Liz goes along sometimes
To relax and read a book.
Better than being online
Or caught on the end of a hook!

There's mealworms and maggots –
For a fish, a tasty dish.
Your meal could be some faggots
Or a nice piece of battered fish!

Time to put your tackle away –
Stop fiddling with your flies.
A rival's caught a tiddler today,
But yours was a big surprise!

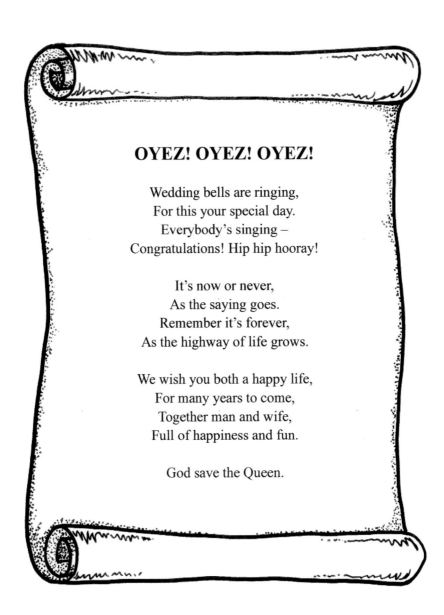

OYEZ! OYEZ! OYEZ!

Wedding bells are ringing,
For this your special day.
Everybody's singing –
Congratulations! Hip hip hooray!

It's now or never,
As the saying goes.
Remember it's forever,
As the highway of life grows.

We wish you both a happy life,
For many years to come,
Together man and wife,
Full of happiness and fun.

God save the Queen.

THE LLANELLI STARS

I've seen you many a time,
Conducting this great choir.
I hope you like the rhyme
For The Dragons I admire.

Llanelli Male Voice Choir –
The very, very best,
Of whom I never tire,
Much better than the rest.

Keeping the choir in control,
Their voices all in tune,
Singing with heart and soul,
You must be over the moon.

Go on, give the boys a fright.
Since winning *The Weakest Link*,
Make it quiz, not practice night –
Something to make them think.

The lads enjoy their singing,
And a drink or two.
It keeps them up and running,
Quite often to the loo.

It lubricates their voices,
Oiled and ready to go,
Like well-tuned Rolls-Royces,
So let the singing flow.

Wherever you go
In the world today,
Keep on singing,
The Dragons' way.

I wish you all
The very best,
Good luck, good health
And happiness.

Ymlaen Llanelli.

WEDDING DAY

It's your wedding day
And you'll be husband and wife.
Congratulations all the way
On the happiest day of your life.

Look at each other and linger,
As you both say I do.
The ring slips on your finger.
Best wishes are sent to you.

Whatever you choose to do
Together as husband and wife,
Hope that path will lead you
To a long and happy life.

GOLDEN WEDDING DAY

Your golden wedding's here –
How the years fly by!
Should we shed a tear,
Or maybe a great big sigh?

When you look back
To fifty years ago,
Would you still say yes
Or would you say no?

Best wishes are sent
For you both today.
Enjoy the moment
In every way.

GALINA AND MIKE'S BABY, ANTON

I wish you all the best
For the happy day to come.
Then you'll need a rest
Before you start the fun.

First baby is always a joy,
If it's a girl or a boy.
With Christmas so near,
It's a nice time of year.

For the birth of a child,
So meek and so mild,
A little angel, a little star
Shines so bright from afar.

CLAIRE AND MARTIN'S BABY, ANNA

It's your first baby,
A lovely little girl.
It's so exciting,
Your heads in a whirl.

You're parents at last –
There's no time to spare.
Always changing nappies
On bums that are bare.

Sleepless nights and crying –
Things won't be the same.
Then she'll start talking
And learn to say her name.

It won't be for long –
They grow so fast.
Then she'll be gone –
It's peace at last!

HAPPY BIRTHDAY, MUM

Now that you're eighty,
Gone are the days
When you had lots of fun
In many, many ways.

You danced to Johnny Stiles,
Roller-skated too.
If someone took you home,
That was a bonus for you!

Along with two friends
You walked round the Isle of Wight,
Got locked out
And gave everyone a fright!

You've travelled a lot –
Now it's r and r.
So put your feet up,
Have a drink from the bar.

HAPPY BIRTHDAY, DAD

Happy birthday, Dad.
You're eighty-five today.
It's long since you were a lad,
Playing snooker along the way.

You were in the forces,
And The Paragon Band.
Now it's domestic courses,
With a supervisor on hand.

As the years have gone by,
You've learned to manoeuvre.
No more DIY –
It's washing-up and the Hoover!

Now you're feeling better,
Who knows what lies ahead?
The Queen might send a letter,
Or maybe a tenner instead!

12th SEPt 1922

THE BIG FIVE-O

Now that you're fifty,
Things start to wear –
Hands and feet,
Face and hair.

Now that you're fifty,
Wrinkles appear.
You're not as nifty
As you were last year!

It's the big five-o –
You're over the hill.
You've lost your go
And need a pill.

Go for a hike
Or take a swim.
Get on your bike
To keep in trim.

ODE TO DAVID SELBY

Good luck for your retirement.
Sure you'll have a ball,
With lots of DIY –
It'll drive you up the wall.

Have a lie in bed,
Leave computing behind,
Do something else instead,
Delete it from your mind.

Plenty of time to plan
A few days away,
Maybe in a caravan.
What will the other half say?

Golf is your game,
So hole it in one.
You've got lots of time –
It can be done!

But don't take too long –
Time's running out.
Just have lots of fun –
That's what it's all about.

LIL ST GEORGE, HR – H!

You've worked a long time
In Triumph's HR.
It's the end of the line
And they've lost a star.

No more sitting on your bum
In that office chair.
Have a drink and sticky bun,
Go out, let down your hair.

You'll have more time,
For tending your plants,
Instead of dealing with
People, paper and pants.

Dressing up for Christmas dinner,
Serving all the staff,
Sorting out the prizewinners –
It really was a laugh.

Thinking back as you do,
Remembering the past,
People that you knew,
Time flies by so fast.

FORGET ME KNOT

There was Hornbuckle, Heathfield, Webb and Wise,
Hazlehurst, Tylee and Booth,
Gone but not forgotten –
Did it really run that smooth!

To friends you leave behind,
Wave and say goodbye.
You've all been very kind,
But it's time for you to fly.

THERE'S ONLY ONE MIKE WILLS!

Everywhere we hear you shout –
What else can we say?
Always rushing round about,
Drinking coffee all day.

What a sense of humour!
"You're joking," we'll say.
"Is it just a rumour
Or are you leaving us today?"

There is no doubt
You caused a riot,
So without you about
It'll be rather quiet!

Many years in underwear –
Now it's time to retire,
Laze about completely bare
And do what you desire.

So have a lie in bed –
Don't think of climbing trees.
You might fall on your head,
So call an expert, please!

We wish you a happy
And healthy life
With not so much trouble
And far less strife.

MOTORBIKE-MAD CHRIS

Happy birthday, Chris.
Now you're sixty-five
Are you still as fit,
Healthy and alive!

Can you get your leg over?
The motorbike, I mean!
Can you still bend down
And give it a good clean?

Next it could be a scooter –
A mobility one, I mean!
Make sure it's got a hooter –
You'll be heard as well as seen.

Be happy and healthy
And keep on track.
Live life to the full
And don't look back.

CHRISTMAS TIME

Christmas time's for children,
So, all you girls and boys,
Go and hang your stockings up –
You might receive some toys.

On Christmas morning
You open your eyes
To see all the presents –
What a surprise!

Can't wait to open them
To see what you've got.
But where do you start?
There's such a lot.

Enjoy your Christmas
Whatever you believe.
Be happy and grateful
For what you receive.

SAGA OF THE BED

We wish we had a bed
To lie our body and our head.
But the smell gets up our noses
And creeps down to our toeses.

We've put it in the garden,
We've put it in the shed.
Maybe something's crept inside,
Sleeping or is it dead?

We can't sleep a wink
With this awful stink,
So it's back to M&S
For compensation, no less!

One day we'll have a bed
That doesn't get up our noses.
It'll smell oh, so sweet,
Just like a bed of roses.

GOLF

Golf is the game,
All bunkers and balls.
Up it goes
And down it falls.

On to the fairway,
Up to the green,
Then down to the hole.
That's really mean!

If you win the next hole,
You're a lucky old soul.
So enjoy every minute,
'Cause you're in it to win it!

At last the eighteenth tee –
The end, after hole after hole.
You're dying for a pint and a pee!
Just for your body and soul.

GAMBLING

Gambling's a mug's game,
Or so they say.
You place your bet
And lose it the same day.

You can bet on anything –
The bookies aren't fools.
There's the lottery, greyhounds,
Horses or the pools.

You're in the casino,
Play blackjack or poker.
Gamble on that,
And you'll be the joker!

Only if you're lucky
You could win.
To be better off,
Put your money in a tin!

MY POPSOCKS

I love my popsocks,
They're woolly and warm.
They go with my frocks.
Sometimes they get torn.

They're all different colours,
Some stripes and dots.
They come up to my knees,
And cover my spots.

It won't be the same
With a new pair –
I'd rather my legs
Were completely bare!

Now there's a hole!
And I've had them years.
My lovely popsocks,
So I am in tears.

RAMBLING MIKE

Off like a greyhound,
Leading the pack,
In leaps and bounds
Away down the track.

When you take a hike
It's for mile after mile,
Along Offa's Dyke,
Over stile after stile.

Through the Brecon Beacons
To the valley down below.
Your legs, they start to weaken
And your cheeks are all aglow.

In wind and rain,
Up hills and down dales,
Along leafy lanes
Through England and Wales.

Take a stroll beside the sea,
Away from the rank and file.
You find a quiet spot for tea,
A rock to rest a while.

Now that you're older
Take the easy way out –
Look over your shoulder
And don't rush about.

Enjoy a ramble
Till you come to a stop.
Life's a gamble,
So go for the top!

MALCOLM WISE

You work for the very best –
Triumph is the name.
They shadow all the rest,
Earning international fame.

You sure know how to organise –
It's what you're paid to do.
With a name like Mr Wise,
There's nobody better than you.

Because you're into underwear,
Of which you engineer,
The ins and outs of how it works
And exactly what goes where!

You're keen on stamp collecting,
From nations everywhere,
Always sticking and arranging
With that organising flair!

SKILFUL HANDS

You're a surgeon in plastics –
I've had some work done.
It wasn't so drastic,
But not really fun.

Greg, you're an expert,
It has to be said,
Especially with needles
And lots of thread.

I don't mean material,
Like sewing clothes,
Just human skin
From your head to your toes!

Good job it's not
Catgut you use today,
Or you'd see the join
A mile away.

When asked, "Who did this?"
The nurses all knew.
It's no hit or miss –
Mr Thomas, that's who.

If you're in need of repair,
Mr T is first rate.
You go in worse for wear,
But come out looking great!

TEDDY-BOY TED:
RETIREMENT FROM TRIUMPH!

Enjoy your retirement,
With time to spare
For cooking, cleaning
And washing your hair!

Out of ladies' underwear –
That's all in the past.
Now you feel much better,
You've never moved so fast.

You rock and roll,
And jive as well.
Look at the legs –
Can't you tell?

You rush to the pub
For a pint and some grub.
Time doesn't matter –
Sit down, relax and get fatter.

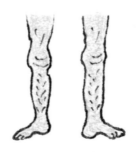

MARION, THE WHIRLWIND

It's time for the whirlwind
To slow down and retire.
Relax and unwind,
Sit down by the fire.

Stop running around
In leaps and bounds.
Be calm and still –
Have a drink and a pill!

Without a doubt,
We'll miss you about.
You're always busy,
Making us dizzy.

But never fear,
We'll shed a tear.
Stand up and shout –
Triumph's put the whirlwind out!

JOKER JIM

Your time at Triumph
Has come to an end –
No more jokes
To drive us round the bend.

Strutting around,
Papers in hand,
Looking for something
With your head in the sand!

We'll miss Joker Jim,
As funny as it sounds.
It'll be pretty grim
Not having you around.

We send our best wishes
And won't make a fuss.
Just remember this:
Happy Easter and merry Christmas!

IRISH MARY: LEAVING SLF FILE CO.

We're sorry to see you go,
For you always caused a riot
And we'll all miss you so.
But gosh, won't it be quiet!

How could we forget
When you took us by storm!
But that was your style –
You were always on form.

After twelve long years
We got used to your ways
And need not have feared –
They were mostly good days.

There were good times and bad
In the years that have passed,
And we're all very sad
To say goodbye at last!

PIANO MAN: VINCENT BILLINGTON

It was a pleasure to hear you play
On board the *Oriana*,
As we sailed upon our way
With some beautiful piano.

Some great composers like
Beethoven, Brahms and Bach,
Edvard Grieg and Rachmaninov,
Chopin, Schubert and Schumann,
Not to mention Rimsky-Korsakov!

To play with your ability,
Their music lives on,
Bringing peace and tranquillity
Long after they've gone!

COUSIN CAROLE

Not another birthday –
Three score years and ten.
So let's celebrate today –
Time ticks by like Big Ben!

You used to be a teacher,
And spent some time in class.
Some of them were clever;
Some were a pain in the a—!

They keep you on the go –
Your cats, they're lots of fun.
They have nine lives, you know,
But you have only one.

The piano is your love,
And the organ too.
I hope there's one above –
Maybe Chopin will play for you!

We wish you happy birthday.
Have lots of fun.
Hope good health and happiness
Are all rolled into one!

SANDRA'S CALLING

Congratulations all the way –
You found the path you're after.
Every day's a different day –
Some sadness, fun and laughter.

You never lost sight
Of your heavenly dream
To be a guiding light
And part of the team.

Now you can reach
To the people today,
Stand up and preach
What the Lord has to say.

Remember life's a test,
Not always what it seems.
So I wish you all the best
To follow your life's dream.

MISS YOU, MUM AND DAD

I miss you, Mum and Dad.
There's just the empty chairs.
When I am feeling sad
I wish that you were there.

Just for a while,
I wish I could see
You laugh and smile,
But it's not to be!

Until we meet again,
I'll try not to be sad.
In my thoughts you will remain.
Till then, I'll miss you, Mum and Dad.

ALWAYS
IN MY THOUGHTS.